ACK RIDGE

ork only in loops indicated by arrows *(Fig. 2)*.

Fig. 2

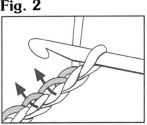

RONT LOOP ONLY

ork only in loop(s) indicated by arrow *(Fig. 3)*.

Fig. 3

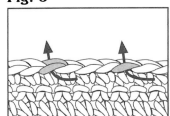

REE LOOPS OF A CHAIN

hen instructed to work in free loop(s) of a chain, work loop(s) indicated by arrow *(Figs. 4a or b)*.

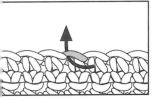

ig. 4a

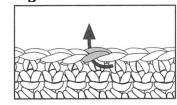

Fig. 4b

REE LOOPS OF A STITCH

fter working in Front Loops Only on a row, there will e a ridge of unused loops. These are called the free oops. Later, when instructed to work in free loops of the ame row, work in these loops *(Fig. 5)*.

Fig. 5

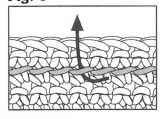

CHANGING COLORS

Insert hook in stit drop yarn, with n on hook *(Fig. 6)*.

Fig.

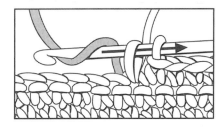

FRENCH KNOT

Bring Tapestry needle up at 1. Wrap floss around needle desired number of times and insert needle at 2, holding end of floss with non-stitching fingers *(Fig. 7)*. Tighten knot; then pull needle through, holding floss until it must be released.

Fig. 7

STRAIGHT STITCH

Straight Stitch is just what the name implies, a single, straight stitch. With Tapestry needle, come up at 1 and go down at 2 *(Fig. 8)*.

Fig. 8

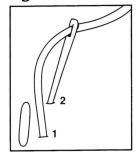

SOCK MONKEY

Finished Size: 23" tall

MATERIALS
Sport Weight Yarn for **one** Monkey:
    Ecru - 5 ounces, (140 grams, 500 yards)
    Tan - 3 ounces, (90 grams, 300 yards)
    Red - ½ ounce, (15 grams, 50 yards)
Crochet hook, size F (3.75 mm) **or** size needed
    for gauge
Polyester fiberfill
½ " Black buttons (with 4 holes) - 2
Black embroidery floss
Tapestry needle
Yarn needle

Monkey is worked holding two strands of Ecru together, **or** one strand of Ecru **and** one strand of Tan, **or** two strands of Red.

GAUGE: 8 sc and 8 rows = 2"

Gauge Swatch: 2" square
Ch 9 **loosely**.
Row 1: Sc in second ch from hook and in each ch across: 8 sc.
Rows 2-8: Ch 1, turn; sc in each sc across.
Finish off.

STITCH GUIDE

BEGINNING DECREASE
Pull up a loop in first 2 sc, YO and draw through all 3 loops on hook **(counts as one sc)**.

DECREASE
Pull up a loop in next 2 sc, YO and draw through all 3 loops on hook **(counts as one sc)**.

CHANGING COLORS
When changing colors, work the last sc at the end of the rnd to within one step of completion, drop one strand of yarn and pick up new strand, holding both strands together, YO and draw through all loops on hook **(Fig. 6, page 2)**. Cut dropped strand and work over ends.

EAR (Make 2)
With one strand of Ecru and one strand of Tan, ch 5 **loosely**; place marker in second ch from hook for st placement.

Row 1: Sc in back ridge of second ch from hook and each ch across **(Fig. 2, page 2)**: 4 sc.

Row 2 (Right side)**:** Ch 1, turn; 2 sc in first sc, sc in next 2 sc, 2 sc in last sc: 6 sc.

Note: Loop a short piece of yarn around any stitch to mark Row 2 as **right** side.

Rows 3 and 4: Ch 1, turn; sc in each sc across.

Row 5: Ch 1, turn; sc in first sc, decrease twice, sc in last sc: 4 sc.

Row 6: Ch 1, turn; work beginning decrease, sc in ne sc, slip st in last sc; finish off.

MOUTH
Row 1: With 2 strands of Red, ch 2, sc in second ch from hook.

Row 2 (Right side)**:** Ch 1, turn; 2 sc in next sc: 2 sc.

Note: Loop a short piece of yarn around any stitch to mark Row 2 as **right** side.

Row 3: Ch 1, turn; 2 sc in first sc, sc in last sc: 3 sc.

Rows 4-12: Ch 1, turn; sc in each sc across.

Row 13: Ch 1, turn; work beginning decrease, sc in la sc: 2 sc.

Row 14: Ch 1, turn; work beginning decrease; finish off.

MUZZLE
Rnd 1: With **right** side of Mouth facing and working i end of rows, skip Row 14 and join 2 strands of Ecru wit sc in Row 13 **(Fig. 1, page 1)**; sc in next 11 rows, ch 5 **loosely**, skip last row, working on opposite side, s in Row 2 and in next 11 rows, ch 5 **loosely**; join with slip st to first sc: 24 sc.

Rnd 2: Ch 1, sc in same st and in next 11 sc, working in **front** of next ch-5, 3 sc in free loop of ch **(Fig. 4a, page 2)** at base of sc on Row 1 of Mouth, sc in next 12 sc on Muzzle, working in **front** of next ch-5, 3 sc in skipped sc on Row 14 of Mouth; join with slip st to first sc on Muzzle: 30 sc.

Rnd 3: Ch 1, sc in same st and in next 12 sc, 3 sc in next sc, sc in next 14 sc, 3 sc in next sc, sc in last sc; join with slip st to first sc: 34 sc.

Rnd 4: Ch 1, sc in same st and in next 12 sc, place marker in last sc made for st placement, sc in each sc around; join with slip st to first sc, finish off.

Weave Red ends into **wrong** side of Mouth to shape corner of Mouth and to avoid Red ends showing through Ecru on Muzzle *(see Hints, page 1)*.

ARM (Make 2)

Rnd 1 (Right side)**:** With 2 strands of Ecru, ch 2, 5 sc in second ch from hook; do **not** join, place marker *(see Markers, page 1)*.

Rnd 2: 2 Sc in each sc around: 10 sc.

Rnd 3: (Sc in next 4 sc, 2 sc in next sc) twice: 12 sc.

Stuff Arm firmly with polyester fiberfill as you work.

Rnds 4-20: Sc in each sc around.

Rnd 21: Sc in each sc around changing one strand of Ecru to one strand of Tan at end of rnd.

Rnds 22-39: Sc in each sc around.

Rnd 40: Sc in each sc around; slip st in next sc, finish off.

PATCH (Make 2)

With 2 strands of Red, ch 4 **loosely**.

Row 1 (Wrong side)**:** Sc in second ch from hook and in each ch across: 3 sc.

Note: Loop a short piece of yarn around the **back** of any stitch to mark **right** side.

Rows 2 and 3: Ch 1, turn; sc in each sc across.

Row 4: Ch 1, turn; sc in first sc, decrease: 2 sc.

Row 5: Ch 1, turn; work beginning decrease; finish off.

TAIL

Rnd 1 (Right side)**:** With 2 strands of Ecru, ch 2, 5 sc in second ch from hook; do **not** join, place marker.

Rnd 2: 2 Sc in each sc around: 10 sc.

Rnd 3: (Sc in next 4 sc, 2 sc in next sc) twice: 12 sc.

Stuff Tail firmly with polyester fiberfill as you work.

Rnds 4-20: Sc in each sc around.

Rnd 21: Sc in each sc around changing one strand of Ecru to one strand of Tan at end of rnd.

Rnds 22-62: Sc in each sc around.

Rnd 63: Sc in each sc around changing one strand of Tan to one strand of Ecru at end of rnd; do **not** finish off and do **not** remove marker.

BOTTOM

Rnd 1: Holding first Patch and Tail with **right** sides together, working in free loops of beginning ch on Patch and through **both** thicknesses, sc in next sc, 3 sc in next sc, sc in next sc; 2 sc in next sc on Tail, sc in next sc, 2 sc in next sc; holding second Patch and Tail with **right** sides together, working in free loops of beginning ch on Patch and through **both** thicknesses, sc in next sc, 3 sc in next sc, sc in next sc; 2 sc in next sc on Tail, sc in next sc, 2 sc in next sc: 20 sc.

Work in end of rows on Patches and in sc on Bottom.

Rnd 2: ★ Sc in first row on Patch, skip next sc on Bottom (behind Patch), sc in next sc, 3 sc in next sc, sc in next sc, sc in end of same row on Patch, skip next sc on Bottom, sc in next 5 sc; repeat from ★ once **more**: 24 sc.

Rnd 3: Sc in next sc and in end of next row on Patch, skip next sc on Bottom (behind Patch), sc in next sc, 3 sc in next sc, sc in next sc, sc in end of same row on Patch, skip next sc on Bottom (behind Patch), sc in next 7 sc and in end of next row on Patch, skip next sc on Bottom (behind Patch), sc in next sc, 3 sc in next sc, sc in next sc, sc in end of same row on Patch, skip next sc on Bottom (behind Patch), sc in next 6 sc: 28 sc.

Rnd 4: Sc in next 2 sc and in end of next row on Patch, skip next sc on Bottom (behind Patch), sc in next sc, 3 sc in next sc, sc in next sc, sc in end of same row on Patch, skip next sc on Bottom (behind Patch), sc in next 9 sc and in end of next row on Patch, skip next sc on Bottom (behind Patch), sc in next sc, 3 sc in next sc, sc in next sc, sc in end of same row on Patch, skip next sc on Bottom (behind Patch), sc in next 7 sc: 32 sc.

Rnd 5: Sc in next 3 sc and in end of next row on Patch, skip next sc on Bottom (behind Patch), sc in next sc, 3 sc in sc at point of same Patch, skip next sc on Bottom (behind Patch), sc in next sc and in end of next row on same Patch, skip next sc on Bottom (behind Patch), sc in next 11 sc and in end of next row on Patch, skip next sc on Bottom (behind Patch), sc in next sc, 3 sc in sc at point of same Patch, skip next sc on Bottom (behind Patch), sc in next sc and in end of next row on same Patch, skip next sc on Bottom (behind Patch), sc in next 8 sc: 36 sc.

Rnd 6: Sc in next 6 sc, 3 sc in next sc, sc in next 17 sc, 3 sc in next sc, sc in next 11 sc; slip st in next sc, finish off: 40 sc.

Continued on page 5.

4

LEG (Make 2)

Rnd 1 (Right side)**:** With 2 strands of Ecru, ch 2, 6 sc in second ch from hook; do **not** join, place marker.

Rnd 2: 2 Sc in each sc around: 12 sc.

Rnd 3: (Sc in next 2 sc, 2 sc in next sc) around: 16 sc.

Stuff Leg firmly with polyester fiberfill as you work.

Rnds 4-20: Sc in each sc around.

Rnd 21: Sc in each sc around changing one strand of Ecru to one strand of Tan at end of rnd.

Rnds 22-41: Sc in each sc around.

Rnd 42: Sc in each sc around; for first Leg **only**, slip st in next sc and finish off.

BODY

Rnd 1: Sc in next 8 sc, ch 2 (joining ch), sc in same st as slip st on next Leg and in next 15 sc, sc in next 2 chs of joining ch, sc in next 8 sc on first Leg; do **not** join, place marker: 34 sc.

Rnd 2: 2 Sc in next sc, sc in next 7 sc, sc in free loop of next 2 chs and in next 7 sc, 2 sc in next sc, sc in next 16 sc, decrease: 37 sc.

Rnd 3: 2 Sc in next sc, (sc in next 2 sc, 2 sc in next sc) twice, sc in next 6 sc, 2 sc in next sc, (sc in next 2 sc, 2 sc in next sc) twice, sc in next 17 sc: 43 sc.

Rnds 4-7: Sc in each sc around.

Rnd 8 (Joining rnd)**:** Sc in next 3 sc, holding Bottom and Body with **right** sides together, beginning in center sc of first 3-sc group on Bottom and working through **both** thicknesses, sc in next 21 sts, leave remaining 19 sc on Bottom unworked, sc in next 19 sc on Body.

Rnd 9: Sc in next 2 sc, pull up a loop in next sc, pull up a loop in same st as joining and in next sc on Bottom, YO and draw through all 4 loops on hook, sc in next 17 sc on Bottom, pull up a loop in next sc and in same st as joining, pull up a loop in next sc on Body, YO and draw through all 4 loops on hook, sc in next 18 sc: 39 sts.

Rnd 10: Sc in next sc, hdc in next 3 sts, sc in next 15 sc, hdc in next 3 sts, sc in next 17 sc.

Rnds 11-25: Sc in each st around.

Rnd 26 (Joining rnd)**:** Sc in next 3 sc, holding first Arm and Body with **right** sides together, beginning in same st as slip st on Arm and working through **both** thicknesses, sc in next 6 sc, leave remaining 6 sc on Arm unworked, sc in next 15 sc on Body, holding second Arm and Body with **right** sides together, beginning in same st as slip st on Arm and working through **both** thicknesses, sc in next 6 sc, leave remaining 6 sc on Arm unworked, sc in next 9 sc on Body.

Rnd 27: Sc in next 3 sc, sc in next 6 unworked sc on Arm, sc in next 15 sc on Body, sc in next 6 unworked s on Arm, sc in next 9 sc on Body.

Rnd 28: (Sc in next 2 sc, decrease twice) 2 times, sc in next 9 sc, decrease twice, sc in next 2 sc, decrease twice sc in next 8 sc: 31 sc.

Rnds 29-31: Sc in each sc around.

Stuff Body firmly with polyester fiberfill.

Rnd 32: Sc in next 2 sc, decrease 4 times, sc in next 3 sc, decrease, sc in next 3 sc, decrease 4 times, sc in next 2 sc, decrease, sc in next sc: 21 sc.

Rnd 33: (Sc in next sc, decrease) around; do **not** finish off and do **not** remove marker: 14 sc.

HEAD

Rnd 1: Working in Front Loops Only *(Fig. 3, page 2)* (2 sc in next sc, sc in next sc) around: 21 sc.

Rnd 2: Working in **both** loops, sc in next 2 sc, 2 sc in each of next 4 sc, sc in next 3 sc, 2 sc in next sc, sc in next 3 sc, 2 sc in each of next 4 sc, sc in next 2 sc, 2 sc in next sc, sc in next sc: 31 sc.

Rnd 3: Sc in next 6 sc, 2 sc in each of next 2 sc, sc in next 2 sc, 2 sc in each of next 2 sc, sc in next 6 sc, 2 sc in each of next 2 sc, sc in next 2 sc, 2 sc in each of next 2 sc, sc in next 7 sc: 39 sc.

Rnd 4: Sc in each sc around.

Rnd 5: Sc in next 33 sc, holding Muzzle and Head with **right** sides together, beginning in marked st on Muzzle and working through **both** thicknesses, sc in next 12 sc remove markers.

Rnd 6: Sc in next 27 sc on Head, drop loop from hook holding Muzzle with **right** side facing and keeping yarn **behind** Muzzle, insert hook from **back** to **front** in next sc on Muzzle, hook dropped loop and pull through, sc in next 12 sc on Head (behind Muzzle), drop loop from hook, skip next 20 sc on Muzzle, insert hook from **front** to **back** in same st as slip st, hook dropped loop and pull through.

Rnd 7: Sc in next 27 sc on Head, drop loop from hook keeping yarn **behind** Muzzle, insert hook from **back** to **front** in next sc on Muzzle, hook dropped loop and pull through, sc in next 12 sc on Head (behind Muzzle), drop loop from hook, skip next 18 sc on Muzzle, insert hook from **front** to **back** in next sc, hook dropped loop and pull through.

Rnd 8: Sc in next 27 sc on Head, drop loop from hook keeping yarn **behind** Muzzle, insert hook from **back** to **front** in next sc on Muzzle, hook dropped loop and pull through, sc in next 12 sc on Head (behind Muzzle), drop loop from hook, skip next 16 sc on Muzzle, insert hook from **front** to **back** in next sc, hook dropped loop and pull through.

Rnd 9: Sc in next 4 sc on Head, drop loop from hook, holding **right** side of first Ear facing, insert hook from **back** to **front** in free loops of marked ch *(Fig. 4b, page 2)*, hook dropped loop and pull through, sc in next 9 sc on Head, drop loop from hook, holding **wrong** side of second Ear facing, insert hook from **back** to **front** in free loops of first ch (third ch from marked ch), hook dropped loop and pull through, sc in next 4 sc on Head, drop loop from hook, keeping yarn **behind** Muzzle, insert hook from **back** to **front** in next sc on Muzzle, hook dropped loop and pull through, sc in next 2 sc on Head (behind Muzzle), drop loop from hook, skip next 14 sc on Muzzle, insert hook from **front** to **back** in next sc, hook dropped loop and pull through.

Rnd 10: Sc in next 4 sc on Head, drop loop from hook, with **right** side of Ear facing, insert hook from **back** to **front** in free loops of next ch, hook dropped loop and pull through, sc in next 19 sc on Head, drop loop from hook, with **wrong** side of Ear facing, insert hook from **back** to **front** in free loops of next ch, hook dropped loop and pull through, sc in next 4 sc on Head, drop loop from hook, keeping yarn **behind** Muzzle, insert hook from **back** to **front** in next sc on Muzzle, hook dropped loop and pull through, sc in next 12 sc on Head (behind Muzzle), drop loop from hook, skip next 12 sc on Muzzle, insert hook from **front** to **back** in next sc, hook dropped loop and pull through.

Rnd 11: Sc in next 4 sc on Head, drop loop from hook, insert hook from **back** to **front** in free loops of next ch on Ear, hook dropped loop and pull through, sc in next 19 sc on Head, drop loop from hook, insert hook from **back** to **front** in free loops of next ch on Ear, hook dropped loop and pull through, sc in next 4 sc on Head and in next sc **behind** Muzzle, drop loop from hook, keeping yarn **behind** Muzzle, insert hook from **back** to **front** in next sc on Muzzle, hook dropped loop and pull through, sc in next 10 sc on Head (behind Muzzle), drop loop from hook, skip next 10 sc on Muzzle, insert hook from **front** to **back** in next sc, hook dropped loop and pull through, sc in next sc on Head (behind Muzzle), place marker.

Rnd 12: Sc in next 4 sc on Head, drop loop from hook, insert hook from **back** to **front** in free loops of last ch on Ear, hook dropped loop and pull through, sc in next 19 sc on Head, drop loop from hook, insert hook from **back** to **front** in free loops of last ch on Ear, hook dropped loop and pull through, sc in next 5 sc on Head and in next sc **behind** Muzzle, drop loop from hook, keeping yarn **behind** Muzzle, insert hook from **back** to **front** in next sc on Muzzle, hook dropped loop and pull through, sc in next 8 sc on Head (behind Muzzle), drop loop from hook, skip next 8 sc on Muzzle, insert hook from **front** to **back** in next sc, hook dropped loop and pull through, sc in next sc on Head (behind Muzzle) and in next sc.

Rnd 13: Sc in next 4 sc on Head, drop loop from hook, insert hook from **back** to **front** in same ch on Ear as last joining, hook dropped loop and pull through, sc in next 19 sc on Head, drop loop from hook, insert hook from **back** to **front** in same ch on Ear as last joining, hook dropped loop and pull through, sc in next 6 sc on Head and in next sc **behind** Muzzle, drop loop from hook, keeping yarn **behind** Muzzle, insert hook from **back** to **front** in next sc on Muzzle, hook dropped loop and pull through, sc in next 6 sc on Head (behind Muzzle), drop loop from hook, skip next 6 sc on Muzzle, insert hook from **front** to **back** in next sc, hook dropped loop and pull through, sc in next sc on Head (behind Muzzle) and in next 2 sc.

Stuff Muzzle firmly with polyester fiberfill.

Rnd 14: Sc in next 30 sc on Head, holding Muzzle and Head together and working through **both** thicknesses, sc in next 6 sc adding additional stuffing before closing, sc in next 3 sc on Head.

Rnds 15-20: Sc in each sc around.

Rnd 21: Sc in next 17 sc changing one strand of Tan to one strand of Ecru in last sc made, move rnd marker after last sc made.

Stuff Head firmly with polyester fiberfill as you work.

Rnds 22 and 23: Sc in each sc around.

Rnd 24: Sc in next 5 sc, decrease twice, sc in next 2 sc, decrease twice, sc in next 9 sc, decrease twice, sc in next 2 sc, decrease twice, sc in next 5 sc: 31 sc.

Rnd 25: Sc in each sc around.

Rnd 26: Sc in next 2 sc, decrease 4 times, sc in next 3 sc, decrease, sc in next 2 sc, decrease, sc in next 3 sc, decrease 4 times, sc in next sc: 21 sc.

Rnd 27: (Sc in next sc, decrease) around: 14 sc.

Rnd 28: Decrease around; slip st in next sc, finish off leaving a long end for sewing.

Sew opening closed; secure ends.

FINISHING

Using photo as a guide for placement, with 6 strands of Black embroidery floss, add five or six straight stitch eyelashes for each eye *(Fig. 8, page 2)*. Sew button eyes in place forming an "X" with the floss. With 18 strands of Black embroidery floss, add straight stitch across center of Mouth with a French knot at each end *(Fig. 7, page 2)*.

BLOSSOM'S CLOTHES

MATERIALS
Worsted Weight Yarn:
- White - 1½ ounces, (40 grams, 85 yards)
- Brown - 1 ounce, (30 grams, 55 yards)
- Blue - 35 yards
- Black - 30 yards
- Yellow - 20 yards
- Green - 10 yards
- Light Brown - 2 yards

Crochet hook, size G (4.00 mm) **or** size needed for gauge
½" Red buttons - 8
Black embroidery floss
Tapestry needle
Sewing needle and thread

GAUGE: 9 sc and 9 rows = 2½"

Gauge Swatch: 2½" square
Ch 10 **loosely**.
Row 1: Sc in second ch from hook and in each ch across: 9 sc.
Rows 2-9: Ch 1, turn; sc in each sc across.
Finish off.

STITCH GUIDE

> **BEGINNING DECREASE**
> Pull up a loop in first 2 sc, YO and draw through all 3 loops on hook **(counts as one sc)**.
>
> **DECREASE**
> Pull up a loop in next 2 sc, YO and draw through all 3 loops on hook **(counts as one sc)**.

FLOWER (Make 4)
Rnd 1 (Right side)**:** With Yellow, ch 2, 6 sc in second ch from hook; join with slip st to first sc.

Note: Loop a short piece of yarn around any stitch to mark Rnd 1 as **right** side.

Rnd 2: Ch 1, (sc, 3 dc, sc) in each sc around; join with slip st to first sc, finish off.

LEAF (Make 9)
With Green, ch 5 **loosely**; sc in second ch from hook, hdc in next ch, dc in next ch, (hdc, sc) in last ch; place marker around any st to mark **right** side; finish off.

PINAFORE
SKIRT
With White, ch 38 **loosely**.

Row 1 (Wrong side)**:** Sc in back ridge of second ch from hook and each ch across **(Fig. 2, page 2)**: 37 sc.

Note: Loop a short piece of yarn around the **back** of any stitch to mark **right** side.

Rows 2 and 3: Ch 1, turn; sc in each sc across.

Row 4: Ch 3 **(counts as first dc, now and throughout)**, turn; working in Front Loops Only **(Fig. 3, page 2)**, dc in same st, (dc in next sc, 2 dc in next sc) across: 56 dc.

Row 5: Ch 1, turn; sc in **both** loops of each dc across.

Row 6: Ch 3, turn; dc in next sc and in each sc across.

Row 7: Ch 1, turn; sc in each dc across.

Rows 8-13: Repeat Rows 6 and 7, 3 times.

Row 14 (Ruffle)**:** Ch 4, turn; working in Front Loops Only, dc in same st, ★ ch 1, dc in next sc, (ch 1, dc) twice in next sc; repeat from ★ across to last sc, ch 4, slip st in last sc; finish off.

Row 15: With **wrong** side facing and working in free loops of sc on Row 13 **(Fig. 5, page 2)**, join Blue with sc in first st **(Fig. 1, page 1)**; sc in next sc and in each across: 56 sc.

Row 16: Ch 3, turn; dc in next sc and in each sc across.

Row 17: Ch 1, turn; sc in each dc across; finish off.

FIRST STRAP
Row 1 (Right side)**:** With Blue, ch 2, 3 sc in second ch from hook.

Note: Mark Row 1 as **right** side.

Row 2: Ch 1, turn; sc in each sc across.

Row 3 (Buttonhole row)**:** Ch 1, turn; sc in first sc, ch 1, skip next sc, sc in last sc: 2 sc and one ch-1 sp.

Row 4: Ch 1, turn; sc in first sc, sc in next ch-1 sp and in last sc: 3 sc.

Rows 5-21: Ch 1, turn; sc in each sc across.

Joining Row: Ch 1, turn; holding Skirt and Strap with **right** sides together, working in free loops of beginning ch on Skirt **(Fig. 4b, page 2)** and through **both** thicknesses, slip st in first 3 sc; sc in each ch across Skirt to last 3 chs, slip st in last 3 chs; do **not** finish off.

SECOND STRAP

Row 1: Ch 1, turn; sc in first 3 slip sts, leave remaining sc unworked: 3 sc.

Rows 2-18: Ch 1, turn; sc in each sc across.

Row 19 (Buttonhole row): Ch 1, turn; sc in first sc, ch 1, skip next sc, sc in last sc: 2 sc and one ch-1 sp.

Row 20: Ch 1, turn; sc in first sc, sc in next ch-1 sp and in last sc: 3 sc.

Row 21: Ch 1, turn; pull up a loop in first 3 sc, YO and draw through all 4 loops on hook; finish off.

FINISHING

Using photo as a guide for placement, sew two Leaves to two Flowers and one Leaf to one Flower with sewing needle and thread. With tapestry needle and 6 strands of Black embroidery floss, sew button to center of each Flower, attaching Flowers to Pinafore. Sew two buttons to waistband. Cross straps in back before fastening.

With sewing needle and thread, sew tips of Leaves to Pinafore.

HAT

Rnd 1 (Right side): With Brown, ch 2, 6 sc in second ch from hook; do **not** join, place marker **(see Markers, page 1)**.

Note: Loop a short piece of yarn around any stitch to mark Rnd 1 as **right** side.

Rnds 2 and 3: 2 Sc in each sc around: 24 sc.

Rnd 4: (Sc in next 2 sc, 2 sc in next sc) around: 32 sc.

Rnd 5: (Sc in next 7 sc, 2 sc in next sc) around: 36 sc.

Rnds 6-9: Sc in each sc around.

Rnd 10: (Decrease, sc in next 16 sc) twice; remove marker: 34 sc.

Rnd 11: Working in Front Loops Only, slip st in next sc, ch 3 **(counts as first dc, now and throughout)**, dc in same st and in next sc, (2 dc in next sc, dc in next sc) around; join with slip st to first dc: 51 dc.

Rnd 12: Ch 3, working in both loops, (dc in next 4 dc, 2 dc in next dc) around; join with slip st to first dc: 61 dc.

Rnd 13: Ch 3, (dc in next 5 dc, 2 dc in next dc) around; join with slip st to first dc: 71 dc.

Rnd 14: Ch 1, **turn**; sc in each dc around; join with slip st to first sc, finish off.

FINISHING

Using photo as a guide for placement, sew two Leaves to remaining Flower with sewing needle and thread. Turn brim of Hat up. With tapestry needle and 6 strands of Black embroidery floss, sew button to center of Flower, attaching Flower to **wrong** side of Hat brim.

With sewing needle and thread, sew tips of Leaves to Hat.

Hair: Cut a 5" length of Light Brown yarn. Fold remaining length in half 17 times. Tie 5" length tightly around center of folded strands. Center Hair below Flower. With sewing needle and thread, sew center of Hair to **wrong** side of Hat one row above brim. Trim loops to desired length.

SHOE (Make 2)

Rnd 1 (Right side): With Black, ch 2, 6 sc in second ch from hook; do **not** join, place marker.

Note: Loop a short piece of yarn around any stitch to mark Rnd 1 as **right** side.

Rnd 2: 2 Sc in each sc around: 12 sc.

Rnd 3: (Sc in next sc, 2 sc in next sc) around: 18 sc.

Rnds 4-7: Sc in each sc around.

Begin working in rows.

Row 1: (Slip st, ch 1, sc) in next sc, sc in next 12 sc, leave remaining 5 sc unworked: 13 sc.

Rows 2-5: Ch 1, **turn**; work beginning decrease, sc in each sc across to last 2 sc, decrease: 5 sc.

Rows 6-9: Ch 1, turn; 2 sc in first sc, sc in each sc across to last sc, 2 sc in last sc: 13 sc.

Row 10 (Strap): Ch 1, do **not** turn; working in end of rows, sc in first 2 rows: 2 sc.

Rows 11-19: Ch 1, turn; sc in each sc across.

Finish off leaving a long end for sewing.

With **right** side together, sew Row 19 to end of Rows 8 and 9.

FINISHING

Using photo as a guide for placement, with tapestry needle and 6 strands of Black embroidery floss, sew one button to each remaining Leaf, attaching Leaves to outside edge of Strap on each Shoe.

BENNY'S CLOTHES

MATERIALS
Worsted Weight Yarn:
    Red - 1¼ ounces, (35 grams, 70 yards)
    Black - 1 ounce, (30 grams, 55 yards)
Crochet hook, size G (4.00 mm) **or** size needed
    for gauge
1½" wide Black gingham ribbon - 18" length
¼" wide Gray ribbon - 14" length
½" White buttons (with 4 holes) - 2
⅝" diameter Black Hook and Loop Fasteners - 3
2" Red craft feather
Craft glue
Straight pins
Black embroidery floss
Tapestry needle
Sewing needle and thread

GAUGE: 9 sc and 9 rows = 2½"

Gauge Swatch: 2½" square
Ch 10 **loosely**.
Row 1: Sc in second ch from hook and in each ch
across: 9 sc.
Rows 2-9: Ch 1, turn; sc in each sc across.
Finish off.

STITCH GUIDE

BEGINNING DECREASE
Pull up a loop in first 2 sc, YO and draw through all
3 loops on hook **(counts as one sc)**.

DECREASE
Pull up a loop in next 2 sc, YO and draw through all
3 loops on hook **(counts as one sc)**.

VEST
BODY
With Red, ch 37 **loosely**.

Row 1 (Right side)**:** Working in back ridges of beginning
ch **(Fig. 2, page 2)**, sc in second ch from hook and in
next 4 chs, 3 sc in next ch, sc in next 24 chs, 3 sc in
next ch, sc in last 5 chs: 40 sc.

Note: Loop a short piece of yarn around any stitch to
mark Row 1 as **right** side.

Rows 2-8: Ch 1, turn; sc in each sc across.

Do **not** finish off.

FIRST SIDE
Row 1: Ch 1, turn; work beginning decrease, sc in next
6 sc, 2 sc in next sc, leave remaining 31 sc unworked:
9 sc.

Row 2: Ch 1, turn; 2 sc in first sc, sc in next 6 sc,
decrease.

Row 3: Ch 1, turn; work beginning decrease, sc in next
6 sc, 2 sc in last sc.

Rows 4-7: Repeat Rows 2 and 3 twice.

Row 8: Ch 1, turn; 2 sc in first sc, sc in next 2 sc, leave
remaining 6 sc unworked: 4 sc.

Row 9: Ch 1, turn; work beginning decrease, sc in next
sc, 2 sc in last sc; finish off.

BACK
Row 1: With **right** side facing, skip next 5 sc on Body
and join Red with sc in next sc **(Fig. 1, page 1)**; sc in
same st and in next 10 sc, 2 sc in next sc, leave
remaining 14 sc unworked: 14 sc.

Rows 2-8: Ch 1, turn; sc in each sc across.

Rows 9 and 10: Ch 1, turn; work beginning decrease,
sc in each sc across to last 2 sc, decrease: 10 sc.

Row 11 (Joining row)**:** Ch 1, do **not** turn; holding
right sides of First Side and Back together and working
through **both** thicknesses, slip st in end of first 4 rows of
Back **and** in each sc on Row 9 of First Side; finish off.

9